HOW IT WORKS
AIRPLANES

by Lisa J. Amstutz

WWW.FOCUSREADERS.COM

Focus Readers is distributed by North Star Editions:
sales@northstareditions.com | 888-417-0195

Produced for Focus Readers by Red Line Editorial.

Content Consultant: James Flaten, Associate Director of NASA's MN Space Grant Consortium and Contract Associate Professor, Aerospace Engineering and Mechanics Department, University of Minnesota – Twin Cities

Photographs ©: guvendemir/iStockphoto, cover, 1; Anton Martynov/Shutterstock Images, 4–5; John T. Daniels/Wright Brothers Negatives/Library of Congress, 7; Rob Howarth/iStockphoto, 9; GordZam/iStockphoto, 10–11; NoPainNoGain/Shutterstock Images, 12; joshanon/iStockphoto, 13; santofilme/iStockphoto, 14–15; Flightlevel80/iStockphoto, 17; narvikk/iStockphoto, 19; floridastock/iStockphoto, 20–21; Red Line Editorial, 22; Alexey Y. Petrov/Shutterstock Images, 25; rancho_runner/iStockphoto, 26–27; Senohrabek/iStockphoto, 29

ISBN
978-1-63517-233-1 (hardcover)
978-1-63517-298-0 (paperback)
978-1-63517-428-1 (ebook pdf)
978-1-63517-363-5 (hosted ebook)

Library of Congress Control Number: 2017935879

Printed in the United States of America
Mankato, MN
June, 2017

ABOUT THE AUTHOR

Lisa J. Amstutz is the author of more than 60 children's books. Her work has appeared in a variety of magazines as well. She specializes in topics related to science, nature, and agriculture. Lisa and her family live on a hobby farm in rural Ohio.

TABLE OF CONTENTS

CHAPTER 1

Dreaming of Flight 5

CHAPTER 2

A Specialized Shape 11

CHAPTER 3

Taking Off 15

HOW IT WORKS

Jet Engine 18

CHAPTER 4

In the Air 21

CHAPTER 5

The Future of Flight 27

Focus on Airplanes • 30
Glossary • 31
To Learn More • 32
Index • 32

DREAMING OF FLIGHT

Humans have been trying to fly since ancient times. Inventors tried to build ornithopters, or machines with flapping wings. But none got off the ground.

The first successful flight took place in 1783 in France. Joseph-Michel and Jacques-Étienne Montgolfier launched a giant balloon made of silk and paper.

Ukrainian architect Vladimir Tatlin designed this ornithopter.

Burning straw and wool heated air inside the balloon. This made the balloon rise.

In 1804, Sir George Cayley built the first glider. It soared on air currents. Henri Giffard built the first airship in 1852. It was powered by a steam engine that turned a **propeller**.

In 1876, Nikolaus Otto invented the gasoline engine. It was lighter and more powerful than the steam engine. Orville and Wilbur Wright used Otto's idea to develop their own engine. They used their engine to build the world's first powered airplane. Their airplane was made of wood and covered with cloth. A gasoline engine powered two propellers.

On its first flight, the Wright brothers' plane flew 120 feet (37 m).

The pilot lay on a wooden cradle. He moved his body to turn the plane. The Wright brothers flew their airplane for the first time in 1903.

Other people began to make airplanes, too. Airplane designs also improved quickly, especially during World War I (1914–1918). The first all-metal airplane flew in 1915. In the late 1930s, the jet engine was invented. This powerful engine made it possible for planes to fly higher and farther than ever before. After World War II (1939–1945), planes became faster, stronger, and easier to control. By the 1950s, air travel was common.

CRITICAL THINKING

What are some advantages of building an airplane from metal instead of wood?

The Spitfire was a common airplane during World War II.

Today, many kinds of airplanes exist. Commercial transport planes carry passengers or **cargo**. Military planes carry things such as equipment, weapons, and troops.

A SPECIALIZED SHAPE

An airplane's wings are curved on the top and flat on the bottom. As a result, air flows faster over the top of the wing than it does underneath the wing. This airflow results in lower air pressure above the wing and higher air pressure below the wing. This pressure difference creates an upward force known as lift.

Each day, passenger planes carry more than 2.2 million people.

If the lift is strong enough, the plane can overcome the downward pull of gravity.

Most planes are shaped like a tube. This shape cuts down on **drag** as a plane pushes through the air. The body of a plane is called the fuselage. The cockpit is at the front of the fuselage. This is

WING SHAPE

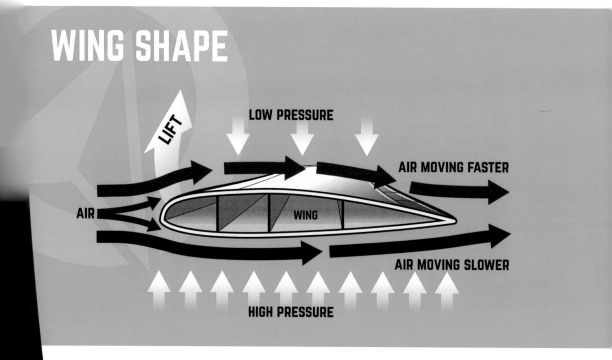

Most planes have wheels for landing gear, but some use floats to land on water.

where the pilot sits. Behind the cockpit is the cabin. It holds passengers or cargo.

The wings extend from each side of the fuselage. Wings may hold things such as engines, lights, landing gear, and fuel.

The rear end of the plane is called the tail. This is where the plane's stabilizers are located. Stabilizers look like small wings. They help the plane fly straight and stay balanced.

CHAPTER 3

TAKING OFF

Engines provide the power to move an airplane. Airplanes can have several kinds of engines. Some engines turn propellers. Others shoot out hot gases.

An airplane's engines create **thrust**. This force causes the plane to move forward. Pushing the airplane's **throttle** forward increases the thrust.

Pilots use an airplane's throttle to control thrust.

15

Increasing thrust causes the airplane to speed down the runway. The plane is ready to take off when it reaches a high enough speed. The lift becomes greater than the plane's weight. The pilot tilts the **elevators**. This causes the plane's nose to tilt up.

The pilot also uses the plane's flaps and slats. Flaps and slats are hinged sections on the plane's wings. Flaps are on the wing's rear edge. Slats are on the front edge. When the flaps and slats are extended, they increase the lift force produced by the wings. This causes the plane's nose and front wheel to lift off the

After takeoff, the landing gear on many large planes folds up into the fuselage or wings to reduce drag.

ground. The other wheels soon lift off the ground as well.

The plane climbs until it reaches its cruising altitude. This is the height above the ground that the plane will stay at during its flight. Most passenger planes cruise at an altitude of 30,000 to 40,000 feet (9,100 to 12,200 m).

JET ENGINE

There are several kinds of jet engines. But all work in a similar way. Fans suck air into the front of an engine. A part called a compressor squeezes the air. Then fuel is squirted into the air and ignited. The burning gas expands and shoots out a nozzle at the back of the engine. This causes thrust.

On its way out, the hot air turns a set of blades called a turbine. The turbine spins the compressor. In some jet engines, the turbine spins propellers, too. When the propeller blades turn, they scoop up air and push it backward. This creates thrust. The faster the blades turn, the more thrust is produced.

Some engines have an additional part called an afterburner. The afterburner adds heat to the air

The gases that flow through a jet engine's turbine can be more than 2,804 degrees Fahrenheit (1,540 °C).

before the air reaches the nozzle. This gives the airplane an added burst of power.

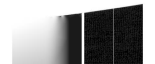

IN THE AIR

A panel of instruments allows the pilot to control the plane's speed and direction. A pilot uses the control yoke to steer the plane. Pushing the yoke forward or pulling it back moves the elevators on the plane's tail. Moving the elevators causes the plane to tilt up or down. This is called pitch.

Instruments in the cockpit display information about the plane's altitude and airspeed.

Moving the yoke from side to side moves the plane's **ailerons**. When the pilot raises the aileron on a wing, that wing tilts down. At the same time, the pilot lowers the aileron on the other wing. That wing tilts up. This is called roll.

PARTS OF AN AIRPLANE

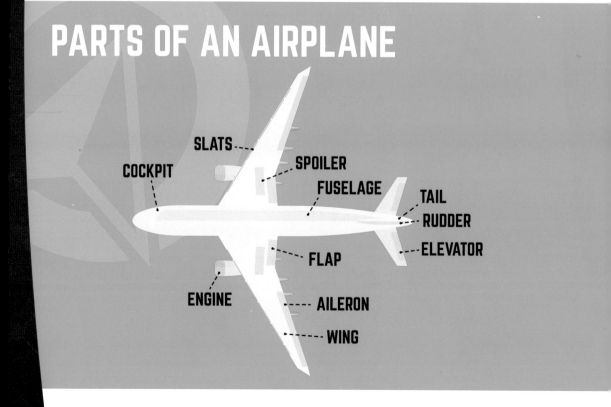

SLATS

COCKPIT

SPOILER

FUSELAGE

TAIL

RUDDER

ELEVATOR

FLAP

ENGINE

AILERON

WING

Pilots use both the ailerons and the **rudder** to turn the plane. Moving the rudder to one side causes the plane's nose to turn that direction.

Radar helps the pilot keep the plane on course. This instrument is located in the plane's nose. It uses radio waves to check for bad weather ahead. Radar also makes it easier to track the plane's location and chart its course.

Some planes have an autopilot system. Pilots do not have to steer planes when the autopilot is turned on. Instead, a computer automatically guides the plane. An autopilot can even control the plane during takeoff and landing.

When the plane nears its destination, the pilot begins the descent. As the plane approaches the airport, the pilot puts down the landing gear. When the plane touches the runway, it is still moving very quickly. The pilot applies the brakes and raises the spoilers. Spoilers are small plates on the airplane's wings. When they are raised, spoilers disrupt the flow of air over the wings. This helps slow the plane.

CRITICAL THINKING

What are some advantages of using an autopilot system to fly an airplane? Can you think of any disadvantages?

After a passenger plane lands, it rolls on wheels to the terminal, where the passengers get off.

Spoilers can also be used to reduce lift while the plane is in flight. In some planes, the spoilers are used along with the ailerons to control roll. When using spoilers during flight, the pilot raises the spoilers on just one wing at a time.

THE FUTURE OF FLIGHT

Airplane technology continues to improve. Materials such as carbon fiber make planes lighter and stronger. Computer screens can replace many of the buttons and dials in the cockpits of more advanced planes.

By the 1970s, some passenger planes could fly faster than the speed of sound.

An F-35 Lightning II airplane can collect and share data about the area around it.

Many military planes could fly even faster. In 1967, the rocket-powered X-15 set the world record for the fastest manned airplane flight. It reached a speed of 4,520 miles per hour (7,274 km/h). That is 6.72 times the speed of sound.

Planes that fly faster than sound are known as supersonic. A supersonic plane flies so fast that the air around it cannot move out of the way. This causes pressure to collect around the plane's nose and tail. Shockwaves ripple out in all directions. When the waves hit the ground, people hear a loud sound called a sonic boom. Because of this boom, supersonic planes were banned from

This Concorde passenger jet could fly more than twice the speed of sound.

flying over land in 1973. However, NASA is working on a quieter version that could carry passengers in the future.

Airplanes cannot fly in outer space. There is no air there to provide lift. But a company in the United Kingdom is trying to build a spaceplane. It would be called Skylon. Rocket engines would propel it from the ground all the way to outer space.

FOCUS ON
AIRPLANES

Write your answers on a separate piece of paper.

1. Write a paragraph summarizing the main ideas of Chapter 3.

2. Do you think governments should continue to ban supersonic passenger planes from flying faster than the speed of sound while over land? Why or why not?

3. Which airplane set the world record for the fastest manned airplane flight?

   A. the X-15
   B. the Skylon
   C. the ornithopter

4. What does the pilot use to make the airplane speed up or slow down?

   A. the yoke
   B. the throttle
   C. the ailerons

Answer key on page 32.

GLOSSARY

ailerons
Hinged sections on the rear edge of a plane's wing that allow the pilot to raise one wing and lower the other.

cargo
Items carried by a vehicle from one place to another.

drag
The force of air pushing back against a moving object.

elevators
Hinged pieces on an airplane's tail that control the tilt or pitch of the plane's nose.

propeller
A device with two or more spinning blades that is used to pull an airplane through the air.

rudder
A part of the vertical stabilizer on a plane's tail that controls the plane's side-to-side movement.

throttle
A lever, pedal, or handle that controls the plane's engine speed.

thrust
A force that pushes air backward and causes an airplane to move forward.

TO LEARN MORE

BOOKS

Abramovitz, Melissa. *Unbelievable Military Aircraft*.
  Minneapolis: Abdo Publishing, 2015.

Farndon, John. *Megafast Planes*. Minneapolis: Hungry
  Tomato, 2016.

Hutchison, Patricia. *The Invention of the Airplane*.
  Mankato, MN: The Child's World, 2017.

Spilsbury, Richard. *Great Aircraft Designs 1900–Today*.
  Chicago: Heinemann Raintree, 2016.

NOTE TO EDUCATORS

Visit **www.focusreaders.com** to find lesson plans,
activities, links, and other resources related to this title.

INDEX

Cayley, Sir George, 6

Giffard, Henri, 6

jet engine, 8, 18

lift, 11, 12, 16, 25, 29

Montgolfier,
  Jacques-Étienne, 5
Montgolfier,
  Joseph-Michel, 5

NASA, 29

Otto, Nikolaus, 6

pitch, 21

roll, 22, 25

Skylon, 29
spoilers, 24–25
stabilizers, 13
supersonic, 28

throttle, 15
thrust, 15, 16, 18

World War I, 8
World War II, 8
Wright, Orville, 6–7
Wright, Wilbur, 6–7

X-15, 28

yoke, 21–22

Answer Key: 1. Answers will vary; **2.** Answers will vary; **3.** A; **4.** B